The Weave of Words

A Collection of Woven Words-birthed from my heart

Urvi Kulkarni

notionpress
.com

INDIA • SINGAPORE • MALAYSIA

Dedicated to my father, my mother, and their immense love for me.

Index

Foreword

An impeccable journey of an outstanding poet has just begun. It feels like yesterday that Urvi, then a 4th grader entered my classroom. She brought pulsating energy with her precocious eyes and an endearing smile. Always willing to learn and excited to know what lies ahead is Urvi in a nutshell.

Trying to read between the lines is what Urvi and I used to love doing in our sessions, and poetry comprehensions were undoubtedly the most engrossing ones. A poet can see the extraordinary in the most ordinary things and that she definitely can.

Urvi's poems on nature are beguiling. "The warmth of her poems heals my sore soul" (a line from her poem 'Golden Daylight). They reflect a deep understanding of life which is rare for the children of her age. There are many anecdotes about my favorite student and her work, but it is time we let her book speak to the readers now.

I wish her pen continues to enthrall readers with her poems into the beyond.

Foreward by *Mrs. Ujjwal Dey*

Acknowledgement

I would humbly present my eternal heartfelt gratitude to Shree Mataji Nirmala Devi, the ultimate power, who has blessed me with all that I've ever desired to be, to have, and to achieve.

I would like to thank my parents, for always being there for me, in every situation.

I would present my gratitude to my beloved *Baba, Dr Bharat Kulkarni.* He has been my biggest cheerleader, my strongest pillar of support, and my best friend, always. Without his support, I would be nothing. His excitement, faith in me, and pride that he dons drive me to reach my potential to the fullest.

My *Mumma, Mrs. Runa Kulkarni,* has taught me to be humble and to love everyone. Thank You, Mumma, for disciplining me, for supporting me, and for pushing me to go beyond my limits and comfort zones. It is her effort that has shaped me into whoever I am.

I would also thank my *Aaji and Aaba*, for hyping and motivating me, supporting my work, and appreciating it to the fullest.

Today, I thoroughly miss *Nalu Aaji,* (Nani) a poetess herself, and *my Aajo* (Nana) who would have been beamingly happy to read this book of mine. I wish they had been here to read my book.

I would also like to thank my *English teacher, Ujjwal Miss*, for instilling my love for the language English and introducing me to the beautiful world of writing. Further, I am grateful to all my teachers in my school, who read my poems and motivated me to keep writing.

Further, *my aunt, Ms. Reva Pandit,* for designing the cover page and illustrating this book, and bringing my imagination to a beautiful reality.

I also present my heartfelt thanks to *Notion Press,* for providing me with the apt platform to present my work and present it extremely beautifully. I would also thank The entire team of Notion Press, who made our dream come true.

All of my family members, for reading my work, and pushing me to write more, and quite often.

I would also thank all those of *my friends*, who have been extremely supportive and appreciative of my work, and their excitement to read more of my work encourages me to create more.

Last but not least, to all those who have read my poems, appreciated them, and celebrated them. Your appreciation and recognition motivate me to write more and write better.

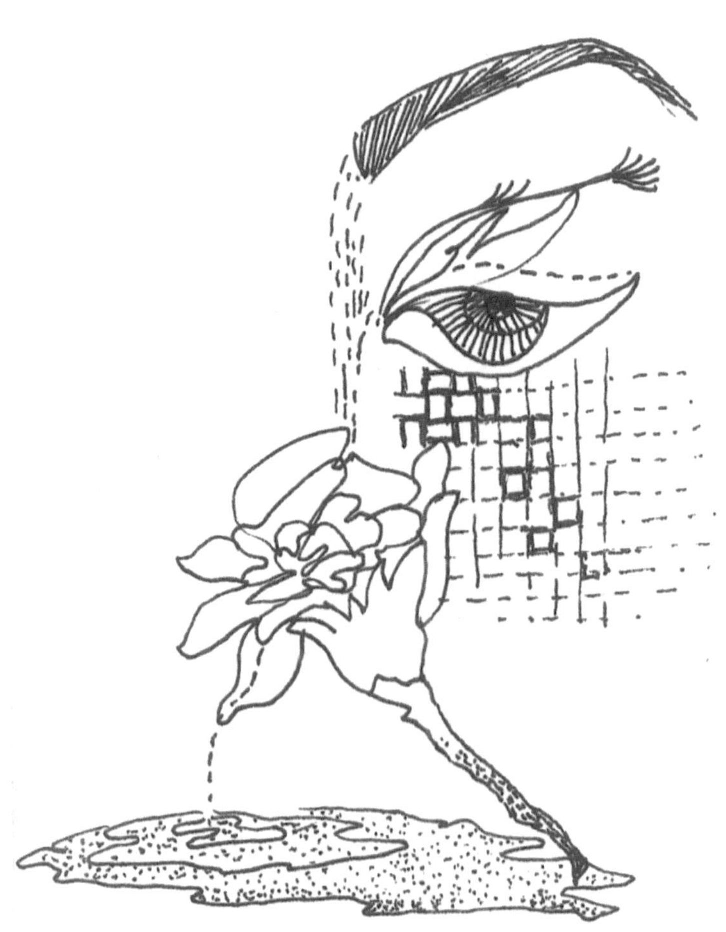

For what I see, I Weave in Words,

My vision is in the poem's eye,

For what I feel, I Weave in Words,

My emotion is in the poem's soul.

Chapter 1

A Haven Weaved

POEMS DEDICATED TO THE BEAUTY OF
MOTHER NATURE

The Day's Elayne

The sun's limbs reached the green grass,
Lighting it up like a glitter-smeared glass,
And I sat there, in the clasp of the sunbeam,
Under the embrace of the giant green tree,
The euphonious sweet chirps of the sparrows,
Reverberated, and shunned all the sorrows,
I sat there, in the ethereal charm of nature
Adorned with Elayne and Twinkle's ornature,
I was between the flying butterfly's flutter,
Aloof from the loud city's pace and clutter,
Then, the sun dipped below the horizon
As the tiring long day now dies in,
The blue welkin was then pink-painted,
And the hearts were very full and elated!!

Pure Bliss

The azure's pure bliss' exuberance,
Spills on the Earth's mundanities,
The blue roof's tranquil soul,
Projects upon the land's normality,
The Essence of the Sky is blessed,
Yet the energy of the Sky blesses,
The lands-brown and green,
That swings and sways with utter glee!

An Evening Stroll

As I walked through the streets of my town,
The lights turned pink as the sun goes down,
Beneath the infinite pinkish sky,
I walked in the solace of life,
As the air smelt fresher than ever,
The lights turned brighter than ever,
The vehicle's bustle zoned out,
As nature then, took over the town,
And I walked with a fresh and new mind,
As the cool wind now embraced me like its own child!

Golden Daylight

In the Daylight my heart blooms,
Its golden charm captivates my vision
Beneath the golden sheath of the sun's rays,
My soul bathes in its warm embrace,
The warmth soothes my sore soul,
And luxury is what evocates the gold,
The golden star symbolizes permanence,
Of hope, tranquility, and endurance,
And of how Nature loves and blesses,
Warmth, security, and imbued silence!!!

January Sunlight

Faint January sunlight,
Glazing flowers in daylight,
A Misty January Zephyr,
Apricating chilly weather,
Beside that coffee table,
At tea time I snuggly sit here,
To take in the joy,
As much as January has to offer

My Reverie

Here, I sit with my legs crossed,
On a rock drenched in water salt,
The water of the sea dashed and splashed,
As I witnessed their peaceful dance,
The sea's salty air and the waves flair,
Was all my heart needed again and again,
But then my reverie broke into pieces,
Leaving behind my solace and peace!

Nature's Irenic Beauty

There was just greenery,
As far as my eyes could see,
The sweet gentle Zephyr's whiff,
Was peace in the valley's rift,
The lush green lands, clear blue welkin,
Seemed better than the lands of Cherubin,
The limpid lake in the lap of Mounts,
Was a sheer feeling of solace around,
The air was misty and the strong petrichor,
Was smelt as it poured on the green floor,
How I strongly wish I could stay there forever,
As the thought of it fills my heart with cheer.

Soil And Water

The earth's sunburned thirsty soil,
Was wearied of the Sun's treacherous toil,
As It desperately yearned for the aid of the cool rain,
The welkin's water too growled there up in vain,
Then The blue welkin's water rushed down,
To meet the anguished earthly ground,
As soon as the soil and water met,
The sky too relished the fete,
The very essence of Petrichor,
Pumped joy into nature,
And my heart was rewarded with immense joy,
From the unconditional nature anigh

That evening

That gleeful pink evening,
The rains waltzed with the winds,
As they twirled around the trees,
The air smelt of Petrichor and their love,
That flowed freely in the cool breeze,
That love brought by a sudden freshness,
In that pink evening that was set with ease!

The Day's Halt

In the sheer darkness of night,
The crescent moon gleamed bright,
The chilly winds twirled and wheed,
Around the mighty tall trees,
That wobbled and quivered,
On the waft of the flowing river,
The watercourse being a mirror,
To the crescent that was a charmer,
Of the effulgent close of the day,
When the time halts every day,
And nature plays her own melody,
Making the night an affordable luxury,
For the selenophile to solemnly gaze,
At the stars and moon's white rays!!

The Daybreak

Just before the sunlight is about to fract,
Nature gives us time to interact,
With itself, with ourselves,
with thyself, with myself,
To meticulously seek within and around,
The elysian Beauty of nature abound,
The dawn is nature's plexure,
It has woven with utter pleasure,
Cool and calm as the morning mist,
Hushed and quiet as a nature's whist,
And then breaks the faint morning gleam,
The sun showers its golden threads' stream,
That swiftly pierces through the white cotton clouds,
And reaches all of the green and the barren grounds,
The sea bathes in the afresh sunlight,
The trees balter in the afresh sunlight,
The birds fledge in the afresh sunlight,
The world wakes in the afresh sunlight,
The day and dawn elide,
The solitude slips aside,
And an awaiting unripe day begins,
With happy eyes and smiling grins!!

The Evening Sky

The evening sky pulls an orange tinge over,
As the sun goes off for a peaceful slumber,
And the sparse and mild raindrops fall by,
Like a slight shower of pearls from the sky,
The cold air now delightfully smells of petrichor,
And the winds blow like peaceful dulcet chords,
The golden sky overcast with clouds glowed,
The sky now adorns a beautiful light borrowed,,
From the effulgent moon and the radiant sun,
But now the vivacious Aurelius is spun,
The amber-looking sky turns black and dark,
And the golden-orange tinge of the sky is lost,
To a soft moon that shines,
There up in the dark skies.

The Evening Sky's Clouds

The evening sky's clouds descend,
As the dusk enchantingly now ascends,
The evening now gracefully enhances,
The evening's flair with life and freshness.

The forest's silence

The forest's silence keeps so much within,
The chirping of birds and rustling of leaves,
The growling of tigers, and wheezing of trees,
In this timid silence, life grows and booms,
So beautifully it builds its own divine haven,
Away from the grey and smoky dirt of the day,
Eternally embracing all nature's hues,
The dulcet chirps mix an elixir in the air,
And adds to the ethereal charm of the forest,
That Has all the elements it protects within,
For The forest's silence has so much within,
A plethora of sounds and nature addresses,
To keep this haven safe and blessed!!

The Leal forest

The sun was setting and shining,
The light was fading but twining,
Between the dense woodland's expanse,
Where trees perform a gleeful dance,
The dulcet wind's sound was the forest's whistle,
The trees that stood on the ground like a bristle,
An orchestra performed by the forest's breeze,
Between the clutter-clatter of yellowed leaves,
The sweet abode of the Owl and little owlets,
Was a cozy plexure on the tall trees' branches,
The dense expanse comfortably accommodate,
Tons of deer and black and brown bears,
The limpid lake in the paradise of the untamed,
Stood in the hug of tons of trees curtained,
The simple harmony of nature's art
Was the sheer glee for my wandering heart!

The moonlight
In the soothing dusky night,
While the moon reflects bright,
My heart finds space,
My heart finds peace,
the moon clambers up the sky,
And disperses its ivory light anigh,
Drenching my whole heart and soul,
In the white moon's gleam, utterly pure,
The alleviating moon now splashes,
The black sky in its ivory flashes,
There is peace in the gleaming moonlight,
Of the moon that proudly shines bright!

The Morning Glow
As the lucent sun peeps through the Azure,
The golden sol's blanket apricates the city,
And it loathes the city with glitter and gleam,
The still night now dozes off for a while,
And the hustle of the day begins,
With the bird's resonating sweet Twitter,
And the temple bell's euphonious peal,
With the melody songs sung to God,
And the enchanting sweet aroma of tea,
The fresh morning air fills the city with energy,
And a new coruscant day begins,
With intense zeal and immense joy!

The Rains

The coalesce of clouds hovered and rested,
On the lush green skin of the mountain heads,
Camouflaging their verdant lush brinks,
The welkin adorned a yellow-orange tint,
As the scarce sunlight fused with the sky's dimness,
the moment was captured in a sudden stillness,
And then the sky sprinkled the rain,
Drenching the earth yet again,
The leaves and trees swayed and heaved,
On the cadence of the pleasant monsoon breeze!!

The River's Course

Our lives are but a river's course,
Flowing through terrains- plain and coarse,
It goes up the hill, and down the hill,
And so does life, as it never stays still,
Leaves no stone unturned and untouched,
Drinking the elixir from every shrub and every birch,
The river moves with force mixed with tranquillity,
Beneath the limitless sky exuding intense reality,
It flows ahead as it takes away those waste logs,
And life flows ahead, as it sways away all those painful
sobs,
And finally, it reaches the sea,
Where it now recedes,
Its force and fierce,
It's energy and course,
And halts and mixes in the waves,
Where there is peace and happiness!

The Sea

I sat there by the seaside,
Gazing at the blueth paradise,
And gazing at the sparkling water,
That splashed on the huge boulders,
With utter elegance and charm,
That was so tranquil and so calm,
The salt air carried some essence,
As the sea tossed on some cadence,
That clement sea's cool breath,
Gently touched me as I sat there,
The glowing sun lit the glaring blue ocean,
The occan, Flowing with jubilant emotions,
The seawater silently hushed and spoke,
Thousands of unsaid words evoke,
Feelings of joy, pleasure, and delight,
Absuming all the gloom and plight,
The blue Marmaris sparkled and glistered,
Beneath the sheath of the golden sunburst,
The enchanting scenic view of the sea,
Made me feel elated, flowing with glee!

The soil and deluge

The Earth's soil and the sky's deluge,
Are nothing but lovers that seek refuge,
In each other's comforting embrace,
In each other's consoling solace,
The Earth's soil - calm and steady,
Births precious crops and flowers beautifully,
And the sky's deluge- fierce and stormy,
Holds the power to destroy anything completely,
The tender soil softens the fierce deluge,
The fierce deluge toughens the tender soil,
And the two lovers harvest life unitedly,
On the earth, that smiles delightedly!

The Tranquillity of the Night

The dusky Starry night and moon aglow,
Are Salvatore of the day that goes slow,
After a long tiring day full of drudgery,
It feels calmer as it's the day's recovery,
The twinkly stars that are red and blue and green,
Soothingly take exhaustion away being serene,
The cool white moon hushes and sings a lullaby,
To the oldest of elders and the youngest of children,
The gaze on the cool dark sparkling roof,
Absorbs the discomfort and all of those blues,
And prepares one for a new unborn day,
To face and acknowledge all that is coming our way,
The dusky Starry night and moon aglow,
Are Salvatore of the day that goes slow.

The unraveling sky

The unraveling sky is like a poet's words,
Tender than the sky, crispier than the wind,
It makes you cry tears that are saltier than the pain,
And makes you laugh harder, happier than the rain,
The rain has a plethora of feelings,
Choosing one is my part of dealing,
Choosing the happy one bloats me up,
Like cotton clouds, grey, and pump,
But choosing the pain pierces my heart,
But the deluge tells me to go quite far,
Away from the pain and away for myself,
To enjoy the deluge and choose my happy self!

October Sunshine

October sunshine and the gentle wind blow,
Charming sunlight and the gold land glow,
The flowers bathe in the freshness of life,
As nature weaves an irenic haven anigh!!

Chapter 2

To Laugh and To Live

OTHER ASSORTED POEMS

Thought of war
The constant thought of war stems from,
the constant war of thought,
The war that silently screams in two minds,
Loud enough for them to hear,
but soft enough for others to discover,
The war of minds is the war of thought,
Cause we try to find our superiority in the other's
flaws,
To prove ourselves, and brutally
disapprove of the other,
To validate ourselves,
and brutally vandalize the other,
The thoughts do not cease to instigate,
Instilling feelings of spite and hate,
And blinds the eye and deafens the ear,
It kills the joy and deadens the soul

Winter Frost

Yellowed leaves and winter Frost,
Conclude the year with great comfort,
On the darkest of nights,
The brightest of lights,
That the quite long year gave us,
Is now leaving without much fuss,
In the happiest of moments,
The saddest of laments,
That the long year, that gave us,
Is now leaving without much fuss,
And thousands of memories,
Sweet enough to forever cherish,
Promise us to be with us forever,
Locked in our memories' treasure,
And let go of all that bad in the past year,
And begin afresh leaving that to repair,
With love and affection,
With faith and wisdom!

Color me in the tint of Spring
Color me in the tint of spring,
Cause I now have my wings,
To fly high in my own illimited sky,
And to claim it to be entirely mine,
With my power and might,
To live and love my life,
And to have faith in myself,
To boost the best in me,
I learn to love myself with all of me,
As I now seek myself within me,
And accept my flaws with my glee,
To be a better and better version of me…

**_I thought as I reminisce about my good old
school days_**
The time now takes us on a ride unexplored,
To solitude, to seclusion, and nothing more,
The urge to meet lovelies is uncontrollably robust.
This is where the time is sluggishly leading us.
I thought as I reminisce about my good old school
days,

The classrooms chirped with chitter-chatter,
Now Seemed to mourn as the twitter is shattered,
I wish I could go back and relive all those errands,
And replay the duties and follow the commands.
I thought as I reminisce about my good old
school days

All of the sites qualified with ebullience,
Now heaved as they are caged by silence,
The school misses us as much as we do,
Even if it's just a building it has feelings too,
I thought as I reminisce about my good old
school days

Music

Music is sheer love,
Music is soulful bliss,
I find my escape,
In the embrace of it,

Photographs
Oh these lovely photographs
My precious memories mimeograph,
Bring me back millions of memories,
with friends, family, and my lovelies,
I travel back into the abyss of time,
Some memories sweet as sugar, sour as lime.
Those precious moments cherished,
The joy, making memories enriched,
The lovely photographs bring me again,
those moments that have passed amain.
Some clear, some hazy,
On days that were not so busy,
Come running back to me,
As I adore that memory
Oh, these lovely photographs,
My precious moments' mimeograph

Rajasthan

From the extravaganza of royalty,
To the unending lines of lush fields,
From the fearless warriors' glory
To a simple villager's story,
Rajasthan has it all,
And Rajasthan stands tall

The eminence of the forts,
Balances the town's simplicity,
The calmness of the farms,
Balances the history's intensity,
Cause Rajasthan is painted,
By the green splash, of the rural,
And Rajasthan is woven,
In the pink tinge, drawn from the royals

It adorns the two shades,
It celebrates the two shades,
From the greens to the ochres,
From the fields to the deserts,
Rajasthan proudly stands tall,
Adorning colours, of shades all,

Rajasthan known for its beautiful architecture and the lores of bravery has yet another shade. The shade is overpowered and overshadowed by this extravagant identity of the beautiful state. This other shade is simplicity.

The simplicity in their lives, the simplicity of their lives.

Rajasthan, having the finest forts in the world, is home to innumerable fields and farms. There is a soothing breath in the air of the Rajasthani fields, that adorn beautiful shades of yellows and pinks of the flowers. This much lesser-known face of Rajasthan too deserves much appreciation and voice.

The word, 'Rajasthan' inherently paints a picture of royalty, but in real life, it has a recessive shade too, the specter of calmness, tranquillity, and life at a calming pace.

Rajasthan's limbs balance the state and its beautifully rich culture. And both limbs carry forward the great culture and traditions and create a unique identity of the state, adding to its pride.

Lost

As the *midnight rain* pours,

My mind runs *out of the woods,*

My thought, it's *the archer,*

and my heart, a *mastermind,*

So it goes to stabilize my thought,

And now I'm *bejeweled* and *gorgeous,*

And an *invisible string* now is woven,

How *enchanted* I am by this peaceful haven!!

—True Swiftie

This poem is dedicated to American singer-song writer **Taylor Swift**. The words in italics are the titles of her songs.

The city's shining

The city's shining red-yellow fairy lights,
Are the heaven's stardust- gleaming bright
Like an angel's gentle swish to the city,
Bringing fireflies makes the place pretty.

The City of Fantasy

This city races fast with the speed of cars,
That pace within the city through the roads afar,
It lets you rise above the sky,
It lets you rise beyond the lines,
The rush of the city breathes life into it,
The hustle of the city brings light to it,
Some tediously swedge to dwell here
While residing here is opulence for another,
It beholds the truth of survival of the fittest,
For the knack of living here is a huge must,
Those people who dream of this city,
Those people who live in this city,
Richly diverse, this city is the city of fantasy,
Home to billions of people, my city- MUMBAI!!

The Dam

She definitely deserves an accolade,
For cleaning the house and making the braids,
For She loves unconditionally,
And works every day tirelessly,
For She cooks all those meticulous meals,
Without quavering excitement and zeal,
She works every hour of the day,
Without even demanding a break.

Just once, when she said,
"Today I feel so jaded"
"What do you do to feel so fatigued?"
Was how all of them brazenly replied,
And then she got back to the chores,
Knowing that nobody would adore,
The so-called "gross" household work,
And those duties she can never shirk.

Who is she? She is Mom,
Who would save her child from every harm,
The one who gives an unborn a life,
A joyous life filled with everlasting smiles.
Who is she?
Somebody greater than the greatest beings,
And nothing can dim the love she holds,
For her little ones, no matter how old,
So, she definitely deserves an accolade,
For all that, she does without feeling drained.

The Past Remnants

My heart is completely lost,
In all those paths, uncrossed,
And those marvelous antique remains,
That once gleamed with beauty and fame,
How I admire these canonized past remnants,
That have witnessed the rules of brave regnant,
Those splendid marvels of history,
And the astonishing unbelievable story,
Of the king and his vivacious queen,
And their very famed love so keen,
And that great war that marked bravery,
Of that king's victory who razed the city,
Of all those women who were immolated,
In the fierce fire of sacrifice to be abated,
Each wall there was narrating a story,
Stories of love, passion, and glory,
There was some magical enchantment,
In that spellbinding lovely environment.

The Shining City

When the clouds descend down,
Like a heaven's kiss to the town,
It showers the gentle sprinkle,
And the town gleams like glitter,
In the faint sun's energetic beams,
That apricates the whole of the city,
Spreading shine and rain all over.

Time

The future is a folded wrap of time,
The mystery of which, no one knows,
All we know is the past behind,
And the present that we behold

Chapter 3-

A Piece of Mind

POEMS ON REALITIES

A Restart

Why give, when nothing in return,
Why stay, when everything is in a burn,
Not to give is a much better chance,
Then to stay in the dark, blinded by a scarf,
The scarf is of dark delusion and deceit,
The scarf is a symbol of purity's dirty defeat,
Yet again, life gives a chance to restart,
With happy minds and grinning hearts!

A reveuse

I am a reveuse in this world,
Who loves to live in a reverie,
Amidst the gruesome truth,
I love to amend the reality,
In terms of colours and joy,
In terms of happiness anigh,
To transform my world with fairy lights,
In sparkling days and sparkling nights

A Talk

All speak and no hark,
All noise but no talk,
Because a talk is between two,
And then the noise ensues…

Expectations

Our expectations are the only ones that mar,
Piercing like a sharp dagger in the heart,
It multiplies our worries and complications,
Cause the real fault lies in rosy expectations,
And not in those who we claim to be devious
As the course of life then becomes tedious.....

Grins and frowns

I ponder how a child laughs,
It plays and laughs, and laughs and plays,
On seeing the sunrise, it smiles
On seeing the sunsets, it grins,
Then it grows up, and learns to frown,
It slogs and frowns, and frowns and slogs,
On seeing the sunrise, it frowns,
On seeing the sunset, it whines,
Why does it not acknowledge the sunrise,
In a world full of shines and glitters?
Why does it not acknowledge the sunset,
In a world full of soothing nighttime?
Why does it frown, and forget to laugh,
In a world of colors and flowers?

Hold the Moment

Hold the moment and breathe,
Let the spirit of the moment seep,
In the heart to purify
In the heart to rectify,
All those colours of life not so joyous,
Of which the heart is heavily tired,
To find the slightest of light,
To find the essence of life!

Hope

The world is woven from hope,
As the sun rises and spreads its warmth,
In this world to add the essence of life,
The flower blooms, to add a vivid tint,
In this world to add the essence of life,
And The bird chirps to spread its Twitter,
In this world to add the essence of life,
I live, enjoy and love my world,
Because the world is woven from hope…

I dare to dream,
I dare to dream
And dream to dare,
To strive in this world,
Nonchalant and unfair,
I dare to dream,
And dream to dare,
To stand with my might,
And fulfill my prayer,
I dare to dream,
And dream to dare,
To follow my own energy,
And shine with a flare
I dare and I dream,
To let myself out clean,
Clean, from the dirt of the world,
The grime that malices us,
And tampers our dreams,
Leaving us in howls and screams.....

Intelligence

What is a man made of?

Emotions, thoughts, or actions to execute?

What is a man made of?

Dreams, aspirations, or plans too acute?

Intelligence makes the mind,

And this mind makes the man,

So intelligence governs the mind,

And the mind governs the man.

Life

Life is as bitter as truth and as sweet as a lie,
So choose your options being fine and wise,
And look into the deepest levels of looks so great,
To only find the absolute truth that acts like bait,
To attract joy, and happiness and to stay alive,
To attract love, light, and the shine of life

Lores of Life

Thousands of people have thousands of lores to tell,
Thousands of anecdotes- stories of pain, joy, or of
rebels,
And everyone is a hero in their own rattling story,
And everyone needs a villain to validate their glory,
But this glory fades away when the heart stops,
This glory fades away when the beat of life drops,
And the story is then dissolved in anonymity
And fades away that story, dipped in sublimity........

Mysteries

What it shows, and what it keeps within,
Are long chains of entangled mysteries,
What it talks about, and what it means,
Are series of complicated mysteries,
The secrets that lie deep within,
The secrets that lie skillfully veiled,
In the midst of the tremulous sea of life,
Beneath the waves, these mysteries lie,
At the dark-pitched bed of life,
Where there's no room for any light,
And just the pitch-dark bitter truth lies,
Free from the flaps of delusional lies......

Painting the Sky
I paint the sky,
With the colors of joy,
I paint the sky,
With the essence of life,
I paint the sky vibrant and bright,
With all those colors in life's void,
The red fuming fiery ambition,
The pink warm compassion,
The blue soothing icy stroke,
And the calming green spring's hope,
To balance all life's elements,
I paint what I have dreamt!

Pretty Lies

Happy pictures are pretty lies,
The happy eyes have muffled cries,
For every eye shreds threads of pain,
The pain, as heated as a fire's flame,
That Rises, growls, and forward it leaps,
to burn down the silk carefully weaved,
Of so much love, perseverance, and patience,
And turn it into nothing but an ugly cinder,
In the flame's angry and hungry fire,
Ready to consume the silk, quite admired

Rhythm

Our life swings on destiny's cadence,
A rhythm of life, to maintain balance,
As the beats rise, the lively life breathes,
As the beats drop, life almost halts,
Yet again, the beats rise,
As they bring hope anigh,
But isn't that the essence of life,
To rise and drop, and drop and rise.

Tears

Today again, I saw a reflection,
Crying tears of sorrow,
Those tears that soaked her heart,
Those cuts that sored her heart,
That lingering feeling of pain,
That clung to her heart
Since so many years passed amain,
Yet she is a strong pillar,
To a brother, as his mother,
Whom he lost to ruthless fate…

The Camouflaged Visage

Every heart is burdened with pain,
As it bleeds and struggles in vain,
It belches out sorrowful tears from eyes,
Because of the sorrow of deceit and lies,
But one dons the fake happy veil,
To hide and let the agony conceal,
For the judgy world and easy camouflage,
In a world flooded with such masked visages,
The wounds of the heart are not aided,
But hidden in a mask of happy bandages,
The life seems flawlessly perfect,
But there certainly is some defect,
In the apparently happy hearts and eyes,
In a world of complete falseness and lies…..

The Curtain

All of us are behind an opaque screen,
As it obscures us and keeps us in a shield,
As soon as the curtains are slowly lifted,
Than the dirty faces too slowly lay bare,
Exposing the dirt and hypocrisy,
Yet the world is drawn by flattery,
Then why pay heed to the showy material,
Ignoring the actual beauty that is ethereal,
That actual beauty seeking refuge in flaps,
That actual beauty, purely without any tact,
Then why pay heed to the showy screen,
That obscures a very different and dirty scene,
And why not look at the deeper stage,
Of things that have an ordinary face…

The Invisible Cage

All of us are caught by a cage,
That captivates and dominates,
Our thoughts, our actions, and our mind,
And loathes them with dirt and grime,
What do we call this cage?
'Ego' does nothing but incarcerate,
Our own self, and our own conduct,
And causes it a great distruct,
It asperses us,
It absumes us,
Thus turning a human,
Into an ugly demon,
Shouldn't we free ourselves from this cage,
Freeing our minds from malice and rage,
And emerging as jubilant beings,
Making good merrier on seeing!

The Mask

All of us are beneath a mask,
Donning which is a skillful task,
For what we are, is hidden,
Under the mask of delusion,
The Mask lets never lay bare,
Our true skin, colour, and flair.

The perfect human
Why can't a hero have defects?
Why does the hero have to be perfect?
For every human has a bit of fault,
But does that make one less of a man?
A human is never ever flawless,
Cause the fault is in our eyes,
As we search for an unblemished one,
Which is very tedious to find in someone!

The Truth

The tongue speaks the desire of heart,
Garnished with words that everyone harks,
But truly, the tongue has no discourse,
Cause it's embellished with intentions worse,
The tongue's speech is covered in obscurity,
But, the clear eyes belch out sheer purity,
The unsaid words that the eyes utter,
Clear away all the mind's dirty clutter,
Because the eyes are clear and limpid,
As they ooze the truth out of it,
The eyes can never ever falsify,
Cause the emotions dwell in the eye!

The war of thoughts
The constant thought of war stems from the constant
battle of thought,
The war that silently screams in two minds,
Loud enough for them to hear,
but soft enough for others to discover
The war of minds is the war of thought,
Cause we try to find our superiority in the other's
flaws,
To prove ourselves, and brutally disapprove of others,
To validate ourselves, and brutally vandalize others,
The thoughts do not cease to instigate,
Instilling feelings of spite and hate,
It blinds the eye and deafens the ear,
It kills the joy and deadens the soul.

When I was a child

When I was a child,
The eyes seemed purer than the sky,
The souls looked cleaner than the clouds,
All that life had to offer,
Was acknowledged with hands widened as the eye,
All that life had to offer,
Was acknowledged with hearts as full as the sun,
But now the same eyes seem shallower than the shoal,
And now, the same soul seems mucky than the mud,
The same eyes change, as the seasons pass by,
The same soul tampers, as the moons wane by....

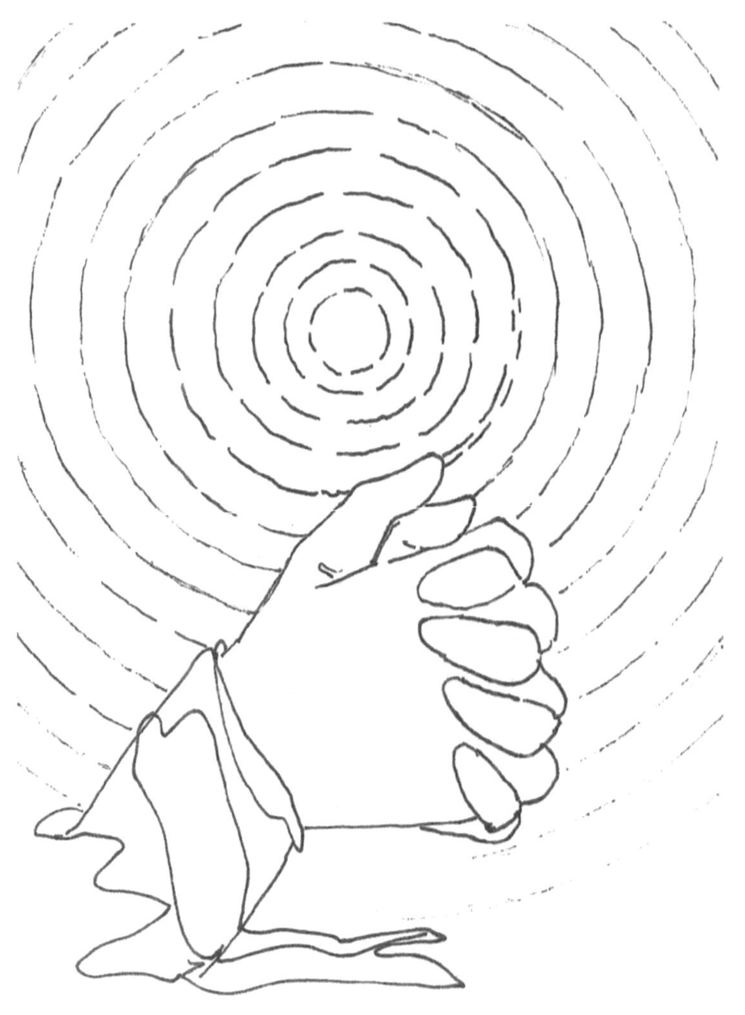

Chapter 4

Praises to the Lord of All

DEVOTIONAL POEMS

The Almighty's World

How I, fortunately, am in your kingdom,
That beholds just love and wisdom,
It is the land where the twinkling sky is the shield,
It is the land where the green grass is the yield,
The green grass- that grows without any condition
This verdant land has trees fruiting pure affection,
They bear fruits of utter joy and peace,
That is completely fueling and sweet,
That fulfills the hunger of fortitude,
Liberating one from the pain and solitude!

Silence

Your silence has so much within,
The silence has so much within,
A gallon full of Grace,
That has blessed this human race.
A gallon full of joy,
That at every moment I shall enjoy,
In Your loving arms, Mother,
I wish to reside forever,
In this sweet blessed air,
I shall always draw my breath,
The light that You've given,
Is my opulence of self-realization,
The joy that You've bestowed,
Is my wealth inflated over the years,
In this last era of my existence,
I shall ask no more, but Your love,
In this last eon of my existence,
I shall ask no more, but Your grace.

Dear Mother

You are a huge banyan tree,
As brawny as nobody can be,
And I am like a small delicate flower,
Under the enormous banyan tower,
And how amazingly You keep me obscured,
From the rain and hail and the furious storm,
Like a mother You love me,
Like a father You protect me,
Like a teacher, You correct me,
Like an angel You guard me,
All I know is that You are the universe,
As You can play with time and reverse,
All the bad and evil happens around,
Because you are the Almighty unbound,
I want to be in Your loving shade forever,
Because I know, there, I will never quiver,
I want to forever be Your little child,
Because I want to be beguiled,
In Your pure love and devotion,
In Your huge vast love's ocean.

My Thought
My thought runs beyond the sky,
The sky, deep and bound,
My thought extends beyond the horizon,
The horizon splayed to infinity,
The infinity, lucid and bright,
And my thought escapes into the light,
The jovial light of infinity,
The frolicsome light of the divinity,
That ceases my thought and brings peace,
That draws joy from the skies yonder,
The curtail draws divinity from the horizon,
Never a loss brings this joy, but this does,
And fills me with joy and Grace,
And weaves a haven blessed with balance!

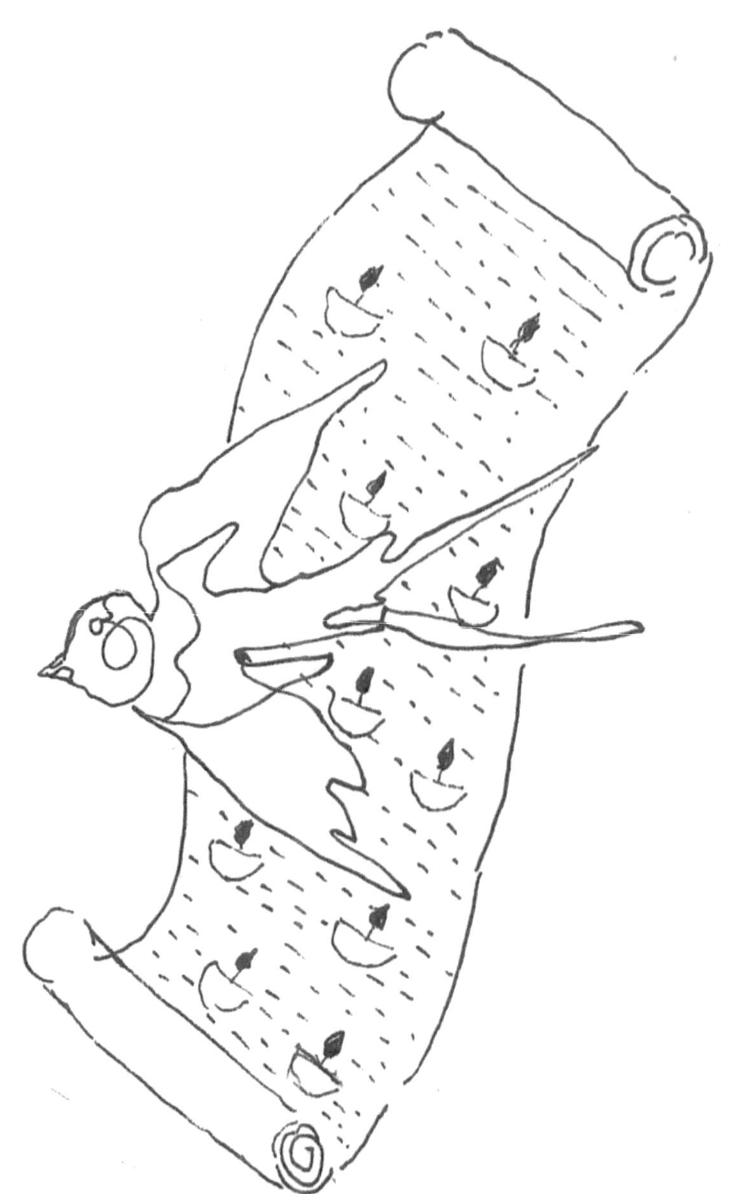

Chapter 5-

To Celebrate and To Love

POEMS ON FESTIVALS

A New Year

It's that hour of the year
When one needs to repair,
All the follies and all the errors,
Looking at thyself in the mirror,
And indulge in brooding deeply,
Of all that thy committed mistakenly,
As the year passed by,
In those days blinked by,
And learn and grow and evolve,
From all the lessons the year taught,
And let go of some of those fights,
And absume the feeling to spite,
For a new year brings much more,
Some new memories to be adored,
A many hurdles waiting to be crossed,
Many new lessons waiting to be taught,
So why carry the *burdens* from the past?
Let thy soul free from this *burden* at last,
And greet a propitious year anew,
Promising just joy gliding through!

Diwali's Lights
Bright aglow, are the Diwali lights,
Like stars twinkling day and night,
The essence of Elayne is ravishing,
The fragrance of the fete is binding,
Glows and flows the aroma of Diwali,
Grows and bestows the sanctity of Diwali!!!

The Indian Independence Day

The world was painted in the tricolor,
The sun-splashed orange on the sky,
The earth birthed green trees anigh,
And in the middle lay the crisp air,
That carried the white peace's flair!

The tricolor that proudly flutters high,
Has so many stories to tell with a sigh,
The tricolour is woven by heart-wrenching sacrifice,
And the pain of mothers and lamenting wives,
That sprouted from their irreparable loss,
Yet all the stories are somewhere lost.....

India's story and struggle for independence are quite talked about around the Globe. However, many survivors, strugglers, and martyrs are still not talked about, even in India. These valuable sons of Mother India were sacrificed for free air to breathe in India, yet we forget to pay them our humble homage to them.

The fete of lights
The air is filled with a fragrance,
Of flowers yellow and orange,
The red Rose's enthralling aroma,
Night Jasmine's magical charisma,
Lotuses are offered to the Almighty,
With a heart carrying sheer purity.

It seems like the stars come gliding down,
In each of the houses of every little town,
As they are lit by the sparkling lights,
And their hearts flowing with delight,
All the houses gleam with joy and glee,
As they now forfend happier families.

Delectables deep fried in the goodness of *ghee*,
Some soaked in the rich golden brown *Chashni*,
Orange Spirally fried *Jalebis* always remains favourite,
And soft brown *Gulab Jamuns* that melt on the palate,
Silver and Copper plates adorn these delicacies,
Golden brown besan *ladoos* and spiral *chaklis*.

Women drape embellished 6 yards of elegance,
And the long frolic tresses neatly weave in buns,
The hands cradle colorful glass and gold bangles,
Whose tinkling sweet sound fills the whole residence,
and The men adorn the traditional treasures,
Flaunting *kurtas* and *Dhotis* with pleasure.

It is that time of the year when there is no room for woes
and complaints.
It is a reminder of the blessings we possess
It is a celebration of the blessings we possess